GATE Theatre presents

\

MARIELUISE

by **Kerstin Specht**

Translated from the German
by **Rachael McGill**

First performed in Britain at The Gate Theatre, London, on July 19, 2004

MARIELUISE

by **Kerstin Specht**

translated from the German by **Rachael McGill**

In order of appearance:

Catherine Kanter	Luise
Joanna Croll	Sister, Schoolgirl, Marta Feuchtwanger
Josephine Myddelton	Emmi, Sister, Moriz Seeler
Yana Yanezic	Mother Superior, Anita Berber, The Danube
Chris Myles	The Soldier, Jappes, Bertolt Brecht
Howard Teale	Bruno Frank, Joseph Bepp
Christopher Campbell	Lion Feuchtwanger, Father, Helmut Draws

All other parts played by the company.

Marieluise is a play in 22 scenes.

Director	**Erica Whyman**
Designer	**Soutra Gilmour**
Lighting Designer	**Colin Grenfell**
Sound Designer	**Michael Oliva**
Assistant Director	**Joe Austin**
Production Manager	**Matthew Darby**
Stage Manager	**Francesca Finney**
Assistant Production Manager	**S J Anthony**
Assistant Stage Manager	**Janina Böttger**
Costume Supervisor	**Polly Laurence**
Puppets and puppetry	**Polly Laurence & Polly Laycock**
Choreography	**Siân Williams**
Set Builders	**Simon Plumridge & Simeon Tachev**

For the Gate Theatre

This translation is represented by Micheline Steinberg Associates – Info@SteinPlays.com, 020 7631 1310

Gate Theatre
11 Pembridge Road
Notting Hill
London W11 3HQ
Box Office: +44 (0) 20 7229 0706
Administration: +44 (0) 20 7229 5387
Fax: +44 (0) 20 7221 6055
Email: gate@gatetheatre.co.uk
www.gatetheatre.co.uk

THE COMPANY

Joe Austin Assistant Director

Joe trained at Hull University and is currently a trainee director at the Gate Theatre. Theatre includes, as Assistant Director: **Protection** and **Wrong Place** (Soho Theatre); **Phaedra's Love** and **Mother Figure** (Birmingham Theatre School); **Vanda** (University College Opera); **Black and Blue** (BAC). As Director: **Roberto Zucco** (National Student Drama Festival); **Skylight** (Donald Roy Theatre, Hull) and **Zoo Story** (Gulbenkian Centre, Hull).

Janina Böttger Assistant Stage Manager

Since graduating from Fachoberschule, Hamburg, Janina has stage managed for Box! Film productions, Schwartzkopff TV Productions and Grundy Ufa TV Productions in Germany.

Christopher Campbell Lion Feuchtwanger, Father, Helmut Draws

Theatre includes: **Flight, Oedipus, Mary Stewart, Dragon, Mountain Giants, Macbeth, Pygmalion** and **The Night of the Iguana** (Royal National Theatre); **The Beaux' Stratagem** and **As You Like It** (English Touring Theatre); **King Lear** (ETT and Old Vic); **Toast** (Royal Court); **Reader** (Traverse); **What Every Woman Knows** (West Yorkshire Playhouse); **Translations** (Birmingham Rep); **What The Butler Saw** (Dukes, Lancaster); **The Norman Conquests** (Harrogate); **A Midsummer Night's Dream** (Globe, Regina); **Purgatory in Ingolstadt** and **Pioneers in Ingolstadt** (Gate Theatre).

Joanna Croll Sister, Schoolgirl, Marta Feuchtwanger

Theatre includes **Habitats** (Gate Theatre); **The 39 Steps** (Empros Theatre, Athens); **Stepping Out, When we are Married** and **Pack of Lies** (Southwold/Aldeburgh); **Shakers** (UAE Tour); **Medea** (AOD UK Tour); **The Bitter Tears of Petra von Kant** (Flaming Theatre); **A Midsummer Night's Dream** (ICA); **Outside Edge, And a Nightingale Sang** and **On Approval** (Frinton). Film includes: **Fakers**. Television includes; **Fallen** (ITV) and **Dirty War** (BBC). Joanna also works as a Movement Director.

Matthew Darby Production Manager

Matthew was born in Manchester and did theatre studies at Salford University College. After graduating, he spent several years as an actor before settling into the backstage role. Matthew was Stage Manager on **The Mystery of Charles Dickens, Noises off, The Play What I Wrote** and **Just Like That, Tommy Cooper** (Tour and West End). As Production Manager his recent work includes: **Through the Leaves, Double Base, Hello and Goodbye** and **A Doll's House** (Southwark Playhouse); **Poe The Musical** (Abbey Road Studios); **Cake** and **Jade Productions** (Tour and BAC.); **Cue Deadley** and **Majnoun** (Riverside Studios). Matthew is glad to join the Gate for the first time with **Marieluise**.

Francesca Finney Stage Manager

Francesca graduated from Guildhall School of Music and Drama. Theatre includes, as Stage Manager: **Electra** (Gate Theatre) and **Black & Blue** (BAC). As Deputy Stage Manager: **The Arab-Israeli Cookbook** (Gate Theatre) and **Age Sex Location** (Riverside Studios). Relights: **40 Hares and a Princess** (Wonderful Beast at Southwark Playhouse).

Soutra Gilmour Designer

Theatre includes: **Antigone** (Citizens Theatre Glasgow); **Peter Pan** (The Tramway Glasgow); **The Birthday Party** (Sheffield Crucible); The **Mayor of Zalamea** (Liverpool Everyman); **Fool For Love** (English Touring Theatre); **Macbeth** (English Shakespeare Co); Hand in Hand (Hampstead Theatre); **Modern Dance For Beginners** (Soho Theatre); **Animal** (The Red Room); **Tear From A Glass Eye, Les Justes, Ion, Witness, The Flu Season** and **Electra** (The Gate Theatre); **Sun is Shining** (BAC Critics Choice Season, 59e59 New York); **The Women Who Swallowed a Pin, Winters Tale** (Southwark Playhouse); **When the World was Green** (Young Vic); **Ghost City** (59e59 New York); **The Shadow of a Boy** (National Theatre) and **Through The Leaves** (Southwark Playhouse and Duchess Theatre); **Country Music** (Royal Court Theatre). Opera credits include: **Coker, Weill, Bernstein** (Opera Group, Buxton); **Girl of Sand** (Almeida Opera); **Everyman** (Norwich Festival); **Eight Songs For a Mad King** (World Tour); **El Cimmaron** (Queen Elizabeth Hall, Southbank); **Twice Through the Heart** (Cheltenham Festival); **Bathtime** (ENO Studio) and **A Better Place** (ENO, London Coliseum).

Colin Grenfell Lighting Designer

Theatre includes: **Lifegame** (RNT, off Broadway, UK tour); **The Hanging Man** (West Yorkshire Playhouse, Lyric Hammersmith, Vienna Festival, US Tour); **Spirit** (Royal Court Theatre, UK & US Tour, Brisbane & Quebec Festivals); **70 Hill Lane** (UK & US Tours, Obie award winner), **Animo** and **Coma**, all for Improbable Theatre. Other designs include: **Playing The Victim** (Told By An Idiot/Royal Court Theatre), **Kosher Harry, Bodytalk** (Royal Court Theatre); **My Dad's a Birdman** (Young Vic); **Heavenly** (Frantic Assembly); **Missing Reel** (West Yorkshire Playhouse); **Breaststrokes** (Stella Duffy/BAC); **Consuming Songs, Would Say Something** and **Bottle** (Guy Dartnell); **Ben Hur** (BAC); **Crime and Punishment in Dalston** (Arcola Theatre); **Ladies and Gentlemen Where am I?** (Cartoon de Salvo); **Stiff** (Spymonkey), **For One Night Only** (Clod Ensemble); **Life in the Folds** (out of inc); **Dog** (John Hegley); **Two Dreamers** (Primitive Science/Design Council). Opera includes: **L'Enfant et Les Sortileges, Le Nozze di Figaro** (RSAMD); **A Midsummer's Night Dream, The Magic Flute** (BYO), **Passions, Charades** (BAC Opera); **The Rape of Lucretia** (Guildhall). Colin and the co-designers of Improbable won the 2003 TMA Best Design award for **The Hanging Man**.

Catherine Kanter Luise

Theatre includes: **King Lear** (ETT and The Old Vic); **A Woman of No Importance** (National Tour); **All My Sons** (Bristol Old Vic); **Tolstoy** (Aldwych Theatre); **Ring of Roses** (Out of the Blue Productions); **Communicating Doors** (Library Theatre, Manchester); **The Servant of Two Masters** (West Yorkshire Playhouse); Work for the Royal Shakespeare Company includes: **A Midsummer Night's Dream**, **Othello**, **A Warwickshire Testament, Pentecost, Peer Gynt** and **The Wive's Excuse**. Film includes: **The Heart of Me** (MP Productions); **A Grey Morning** (Vitamin Pictures) and **A Brand for the Burning** (Skyscraper). Television includes: **Inspector Lynley**; **Cold Feet**; **A&E**; **Casualty**; **Doctors**; **Bugs** and **The Knock**. Radio includes: **A Warwickshire Scandal** and **Straw Without Bricks** for Radio 4.

Polly Laurence Puppets and Puppetry

Polly trained at Central School of Speech and Drama. Since graduating she has worked as a freelance designer, costume, prop and puppet maker. Productions include **Patching Havoc** and **Fall Away** (Latchmere Theatre); **Hamlet** (Greenwich Theatre); **Scenes from an Execution** (Embassy Theatre); **True or Falsetto** (Pleasance, Edinburgh). Television includes **How to be a Man** and **Heavy TV**, both for Keo Films (Channel Four).

Polly Laycock Puppets and Puppetry

Since graduating from the Central School of Speech and Drama, Polly has been working as a designer and artist; her work encompasses puppetry, theatre design and installation. Theatre includes **Teapot** (Theatre Alibi); **Wind in the Willows, Scrooge** and **The Ugh Show** (Jakes Ladder); **Jungle Party Glitterarti** (Half Moon Young People's Theatre); **Elevation** (Wireframe); **October Plenty** (The Lions Part) and **Hole in the Heart** (Theatro Technis). Film includes work for Cop Prop–Boudoir Dolls. Community arts include **Magic Me, Artsreach, Boredom Busters**, The Wren Trust, projects for Barnet, Hertfordshire and Surrey county councils and schools, the Youth Service and the Police.

Rachael McGill Translator

Rachael's theatre productions include **Storeys** (Finborough Theatre, 2000), **Ten Fingers and Ten Toes** (Battersea Arts Centre, 1999), **Round Jamie's** (National Youth Arts Festival, 2002) and **The Lemon Princess** (West Yorkshire Playhouse/Old Vic showcase 2003). The German Translation of **Storeys** was performed at Theatreprojekt Muhlheim in 2001. She has had stories published in **Shorts 5 Macallan/Scotland on Sunday Short Story Collection**, Polygon 2002, and **Shoefly Baby – The Asham Award Short Story Collection**, Bloomsbury 2004. She was shortlisted for the 1996 Gate Translation Award and has translated from French and German for the Royal National Theatre, Hodder and Stoughton and Channel 4. She is currently under commission to The Caird Company/West Yorkshire Playhouse for the final version of **The Lemon Princess** and to BBC Radio 4 for two afternoon plays. She is also working on a play about race and school exclusions, extracts from which have had a rehearsed reading at the Battersea Arts Centre.

Josephine Myddelton Emmi, Sister, Moriz Seeler

Josephine trained at the London Centre for Theatre Studies. Theatre includes **Electra** (Gate Theatre), **Intensive Care** (Soho Theatre), **Best of Motives** (Tricycle), **The Gingerbread Man** (Charles Cryer Studio) and **Missing** (The White Bear). Film: **Cloud Cuckoo Land.** Josephine is regularly to be seen as a 1940s secretary in the Cabinet War Rooms, and has recently been playing Lady Emma Hamilton at the British Museum.

Chris Myles The Soldier, Jappes, Bertolt Brecht

Christopher trained at Central School of Speech and Drama. Theatre includes **Ballard of Wolves** and **Epitaph for the Whales** (Gate Theatre); **A Midsummer Night's Dream** and **Rose Rage** (for Propeller in the West End); **Henry V, Comedy of Errors** and **Twelfth Night** (Watermill Newbury, UK and International Tours); **The Devil's Disciple, The Applecart, Cock of the Walk, Mrs Warren's Profession, People in Cages, Geneva, Cold Comfort Farm, The Schoolmistress, You Never Can Tell** and **Shaw Cornered** (Michael Friend Productions); **Macbeth, Rosencrantz and Guildenstern are Dead, Romeo and Juliet, The Merchant of Venice, Hamlet** and **Insignificance** (Wildcard Theatre); **Coffee** and **The Deed** (Latchmere Theatre); **The Tenth Man** (New End). Film includes **Vigo, The Score, Little Joe's Bad Trip** and **My Flame Haired Beauty.**

Michael Oliva Sound Designer

Michael trained as a biochemist and now teaches composition with electronics at the Royal College of Music. Scores and sound design for theatre include: **Fool For Love** and **Loves Labours Lost** (English Touring Theatre, RNT Studio); **The Glass Slipper, The Winter's Tale** and **The Old Curiosity Shop** (Southwark Playhouse); **Tear From A Glass Eye, Box of Bananas, Witness** and **Electra** (the Gate Theatre); **Knots (in the Dark)** (BAC), **The Birthday Party** (Sheffield Crucible) Other credits include: As well as live computer improvisations with Hannah Marshall (Coccyx), concert works include **More Bless'd Than Living Lips**, an opera **Ocean, Chase** and **Hannah's Dream**, a collaboration with the painter Susan Haire, **The Speed Of Metals, Ultramarine, Cyclone** and **Torso**. His opera **Black And Blue** recently premiered at BAC.

Kerstin Specht Writer

Kerstin Specht was born in 1956 in Kronach, Germany. She completed her studies in Germanistik (German Language and Literature) at Munich University before working as an Assistant Director for Bayerische Rundfunk (Bavarian Radio) and studying acting. In 1985 she studied at the Academy for Television and Film in Munich before starting to write for theatre in 1988. She has written many plays, the most important of which are **Amiwiesen** (premiered Münchener Kammerspiele, 1990), **Die Froschkönigin** (premiered Staatstheater Stuttgart, 1998), **Marieluise** (premiered Stadttheater Ingolstadt, 2001), **Das Goldene Kind** (premiered Münchner Kammerspiele, 2002) and **Solitude** (premiered Staatstheater Stuttgart, 2003). She has received several awards including the 2002 National Award for Drama from Baden-Württemberg for **Marieluise**. Kerstin lives in Munich.

Howard Teale Bruno Frank, Joseph Bepp

Theatre includes: **Tales from a Pier, The Eight Foot Leap, A Family Man, Push, Love on the First Floor** (Union Theatre); **On the Out** (Hampstead Theatre); **Miss Julie** (Haymarket); **Anniversary Sweet** (Finborough); **The Merchant Of Venice** (Birmingham Rep.); **The Robbers, The Relapse** (Glasgow Citizens); **A Doll's House** (Playhouse/Thelma Holt); **The Seagull** (Thelma Holt – UK Tour); **Clandestine Marriage** (Queen's Theatre);. Television includes: **'Mayday 2', Doctor's, Holby City, Eastenders.**

Erica Whyman Director

Erica has been Artistic Director of the Gate Theatre since January 2001. She trained at Bristol Old Vic on the Director's Attachment, and with Phillipe Gaulier in Paris. Erica was awarded the John S Cohen Bursary for Directors at the Royal National Theatre Studio and English Touring Theatre. Directing credits include: **Silence and Landscape** (NT Studio); **The Gambler** and **Oblomov** (Pleasance, Edinburgh and London); her own adaptation of **To The Lighthouse** (Bloomsbury Theatre); **Blue Remembered Hills** (Bristol Old Vic); **The Little Violin** by Adrian Mitchell (Tricycle Theatre); **Fool For Love** (English Touring Theatre) and **Three Wishes**, by Ben Moor (Pleasance, Edinburgh). As Artistic Director at Southwark Playhouse she directed **The Glass Slipper, The Winter's Tale, The Old Curiosity Shop.** For the Gate she has directed **Tear From A Glass Eye, Les Justes**, the devised piece **Box of Bananas, Ion, Witness** and **Electra.** Other credits include **The Birthday Party** (Sheffield Crucible), **A Shadow of a Boy** (Royal National Theatre) and the opera **Black and Blue** (BAC).

Siân Williams Choreographer

Seân trained at the London College of Dance and Drama. Co-founder of The Kosh dance theatre company she has performed in all its productions. Choreography and theatre awards include the Manchester Evening News Dance Theatre Award, Cairo Experimental Theatre Award, New York Film & Television Festival Bronze Medal, Best Foreign Theatre Presentation in Chile. Siân has worked as Movement Director for the Royal Shakespeare Company; Master of Dance for the Globe Theatre Company since 2002 and for all its productions in 2003 and 2004. Other recent work includes performing in Opera North's **La Traviata;** choreography for ENO's **A Better Place**; choreography for RSAMD's production of Stravinsky's **Renard**; directing A Square of Sky for The Kosh, and is currently performing for the Kosh in **Twentieth Century Girls**.

Yana Yanezic Mother Superior, Anita Berber, The Danube

Theatre includes: **Dame Of Camelias** (National Theatre Slovenia). Film includes: **Harry Potter and The Prisoner Of Azkaban**, **Getaway2 – Sony Playstation** and **The Camelion**. Television includes: **The Bill** and **Night&Day**. Various television commercials and voice overs for ABC,BBC. Dance: numerous music awards and videos in the UK, musical and cabaret productions in Germany and ballet and modern productions in Slovenia.

REVELATIONS THE GATE TRANSLATION AWARD

The discovery of hidden riches in international drama is at the heart of the Gate's work. **REVELATIONS** celebrates the unique role translators play in this endeavour.

WITNESS, the 2002 winning entry, was chosen from a staggering number of high-quality entries. The response to this year's award has been equally remarkable, with over 50 entries received from Brazil to Belgium, Latvia to Argentina via Sweden, Germany and Spain. Six of the most exciting and accomplished translations submitted were selected for our shortlist, which were then considered by an independent panel of judges: **Jack Bradley, Penny Cherns, Susannah Clapp, Christopher Hampton, Edward Kemp, Tony Meech and Tim Piggot-Smith**.

We would like to thank the judges, all the translators and playwrights who submitted entries and the sponsors who made the award and this production possible. We are extremely proud to present this year's winning play – **MARIELUISE**.

REVELATIONS SHORTLISTED TRANSLATIONS:

THE LIVING AND THE DEAD by Ignacio Garcia May, translated from the Spanish by Simon Breden *(Runner-up)*

THE BEACH by Peter Asmussen, translated from the Danish by David Duchin

MODESTY by Rafael Spregelburd, translated from the Spanish by Ian Barnett

STA"M by Michael Haruni, translated from the Hebrew by Michael Haruni

NORTHERN LIGHTS by Paul Pourveur, translated from the Belgian by Nadine Malfait

The Translation Award is sponsored by The Goethe Insitute, Jenny Hall, IKB Deutsche Industriebank and Oberon Books.

The Gate would like to thank Saul Avatar, Edward Gibbon at the Almeida, Nick Haymen-Joyce, Tony Meech, Prompt Side, Jonny Ranner, Altan Rayman, Emily Rushton, Whitelight and Rhys Williams.

The Gate thanks its Keepers for their continued support
Rupert Christiansen, John S Cohen Foundation, Charles Hart, Oberon Books, Georgia Oetker, Peters, Fraser & Dunlop, Carl & Martha Tack and Robert & Rebecca Willer.

The Gate's work is supported by
Arts Council England – London, The Jerwood Foundation, The Garfield Weston Foundation, The Gatsby Charitable Foundation, The Mercers' Company and The Moose Foundation for the Arts.

Kerstin Specht

MARIELUISE
THE TIME OF THE TORTOISE

Translated by

Rachael McGill

This book is for Kirstin Fenske and Richard Lean
July 2004
Frohes Zusammensein

OBERON BOOKS
LONDON

First published in 2004 by Oberon Books Ltd
(incorporating Absolute Classics)
521 Caledonian Road, London N7 9RH
Tel: 020 7607 3637 / Fax: 020 7607 3629
e-mail: oberon.books@btinternet.com
www.oberonbooks.com

ISBN: 1 84002 494 1

Cover design by Mark Goddard

Printed in Great Britain by Antony Rowe Ltd, Chippenham.

Contents

The translator would like to thank Corinne Amman, Amely Rudorf and Penny Black for their help and ideas.

MARIELUISE

Characters

LUISE

FATHER

SISTER 1

SISTER 2

JAPPES

LION FEUCHTWANGER

MARTHA FEUCHTWANGER

BRECHT

FRANK

SEELER

ANITA BERBER

DRAWS

BEPP

NUNS

CHORUS OF SCHOOLGIRLS

EMMI

GIRL

MAN

SOLDIERS

ARMY DOCTOR

DOCTOR

CARETAKER

THE LITERARY ESTABLISHMENT

THE DANUBE

A minimum of eight actors can play all parts.

I. A Time in Hell

1. Ingolstadt, Kupfergasse

LUISE: Father makes iron bend to his will
    But not me

    In the evenings he brushes off the rust
    lays the fox on mother's shoulders
    and takes her to the theatre

    I glow with envy
    but they won't do what I want them to do
    They won't take me too

    A red curtain
    between two rooms
    makes an ideal stage

    I create my own theatre
    I improvise puppet shows
    Today the subject is topical
    the sinking of the Titanic

    Entry costs one Pfennig
    The public crowds in
    Even the boy
    who flicks rubber bands
    in my face
    gets in line
    and pays with head bowed

    We need chairs
    more chairs
    still more chairs

    I do everything alone
    My sisters stand there
    like a knot of stupid sheep

The sheep become balls of wool
and the job of the wool
is to let itself be knitted and knotted up

Me
I'm at the high school
despite the high cost

My brother
is dead
I have to take his place

Where's the sea

Who's got the watering can

Who's doing the thunder

Who's singing

'Nearer my God to Thee'

Children drown the puppets in an aquarium.
Everything swims.

2. Regensburg, Convent

The boarding school for young English ladies.

LUISE: The entrance exam was in peace time
but when term begins it's war
The girl's school
is full of wounded soldiers
they're in the gym
they're on the long terrace
above the music room
The girls must hand in their clothes
and wear the uniform
of uniform sacks

CHORUS OF NUNS: The list of forbidden things
'It is forbidden

to wear hair ribbons
Or a parting that is crooked
It is forbidden
to talk in the dining room
while soup is still being eaten
It is forbidden
to write notes to each other
It is forbidden
to carve initials into your leg
It is forbidden
to drop your pencil
It is forbidden
to have a crush'

The SOLDIERS throw down scraps of white paper from above.

LUISE: It is forbidden
to look up at the soldiers
But the soldiers throw down kisses
You have to look up

LUISE picks up one of the notes and reads it.

I've already lost one of my legs
does that bother you
And now you've taken my heart
What am I to do

As the NUNS go past she puts the note in her mouth and swallows it.

NUN: On Saturday baths must be taken
A bathing robe
with a slit in it
is compulsory
Without it you will not be permitted to get in the bath
A nightdress
with no slit in it
is compulsory
Without it you will not be permitted
to get into bed

LUISE: I'm suffocating from the closeness
   that has to stay distant
   Bedstead against bedstead
   chair against chair
   I write secretly
   under the covers
   I write secretly
   after meal duty
   To the tips of my fingers
   I feel the tingle
   of magic
   The dormitory is a submarine
   and I dive
   into an underwater world
   My words drop
   like shoals of fishes
   on the page
   It's an intoxication
   I know
   it won't last long
   The balloon inflates
   and then the air seeps out
   Because of that I only write short stories

3. Regensburg, a hallway in the convent

LUISE scrubs the floor.

LUISE: Where did you come from?

SOLDIER: From the trenches

LUISE: You have to go

 The SOLDIER leans against the wall.

SOLDIER: I can't

LUISE: You're in pain

SOLDIER: Yes
>a lot of pain
>I've had a letter
>from my fiancée
>She told me she only wants a whole man
>That's what I was when she met me
>Whole men are rare these days
>But she thinks she'd rather have one
>who's been shot through the chest
>The bullet goes in the front
>and out the back
>and you can hardly tell
>if you put a suit on over it
>I get rice and milk here every day
>But I'd rather be in the trenches eating worms
>and not have to look down into that yard
>and see the girls walking with their heads bowed
>They don't look up
>It's as if I was air
>The country I fought for can give me a wooden leg
>but it can't give me a wooden heart
>
>I always look
>to see if there's one like Marie
>But now they've all got her face
>I stopped being choosy long ago
>
>Miss
>Please
>Just once
>Look at me

A tear runs down his face. She strokes his cheeks. He strokes her face. The ARMY DOCTOR appears, slaps LUISE.

ARMY DOCTOR: Are you crazy man
>We're not at the front now
>This is a convent
>Those nuns will use any excuse
>to get us out of here

4. Regensburg, Baumloser Park

EMMI: They say Lina met up with one
     She's got a photo

LUISE: I like the lopsided one best
     He looks like he's being blown over by the wind

EMMI: Did you know
     they get injections of morphine
     Did you know
     they're still armed
     If one of their guns went off
     that could really ruin someone's day

LUISE: Do you think
     It hurts

EMMI: I think you get used to it
     Then it gets as natural as breathing

LUISE: I'm not going to get married

EMMI: Who's talking about
     getting married

LUISE: I want to live on my own
     and have an angel
     who visits me from time to time

EMMI: Shall we go and visit Senga Sengana
     the Queen of the Strawberries

EMMI climbs over the fence.

LUISE: It's forbidden

EMMI: That's why

They eat strawberries. LUISE makes pretend wounds in her hands with squashed strawberries and shows them to EMMI.

LUISE: The chastity of the saints
     is watched over by angels

The CARETAKER chases them, cursing, with a scythe.

EMMI: And saints
are not afraid of death

5. Regensburg, Convent

The one-legged SOLDIER throws himself from the first floor to his death.

CHORUS OF SCHOOLGIRLS: A soldier comes flying
nuns sail in
like black birds
and crouch around the body on the ground
In his pocket was a letter to Luise
Luise had Contact with Soldiers
which is forbidden

LUISE: I was just trying to be friendly

SCHOOLGIRL: You weren't friendly enough

LUISE: But I couldn't

NUN: Now look what's happened

LUISE: But I didn't kill him
it was the war

NUN: Luise was the straw
that broke the camel's back

LUISE: I was just trying to be friendly

NUN: Detention
Until further notice

LUISE: I want to sleep
And never wake up again

The NUNS shake her.

Why do I have to wake up

NUN: Luise
    your mother is dead
    You may go to the funeral

NUN: Do you hear us

NUN: Do you hear us

LUISE: Blessed Saint Blaise
    who helps with neck ache
    and fishbones stuck in the throat

    Blessed Saint Christopher
    who helps with the perils
    of fire and flood

    Blesssed Saint Catherine
    who helps with ailments of the head and tongue
    with speech difficulties
    and with the search for those lost at sea

    Blessed Saint Vitus
    who helps with dog and snake bites
    epilepsy and St Vitus's dance
    with bed-wetting
    and with the protection of chastity

    Help me
    even if it's not your job
    Perform a miracle
    Make her live

NUN: Luise
    don't miss the train

LUISE: I'm praying for a miracle

NUN: You won't get one

NUN: Sinner that you are

II. A Time in Heaven

6. Munich, Ainmillerstrasse

LUISE: The dog is house trained
       The room is spick and span
       My heart is hanging out to dry

       I've never slept alone
       A girl used to a dormitory
       Although I was never used to it
       But now I'm so alone
       All I have is this room
       If the room
       were to fall in love with me
       we could leave together
       hand in hand

Shouting from the house next door.

       The neighbour
       has emptied a litre bottle down his throat again
       so it doesn't hurt his wife so much
       When he hits her with it
       Why would a woman marry such a man
       Because if she didn't have him
       she'd break the bottle on her head herself

She eats.

       I'm eating again
       and not crying again
       Plaited yeast bread from last week
       Stewed dumplings from the week before
       Lemon peel and orange peel
       dipped in chicory
       The taste of marinated Christmas

I write
with butter yellow gloves
I write
about a snow storm
and now it's snowing
I write about toothache
and now it hurts
Is it like that for everyone
You call things to yourself by writing them
The good things and the bad

I write
in the corridors of the university
I meet a Red Indian
He calls himself Jappes
He thinks a novel
He walks with me
He bows to street lamps
He hugs trees
I pull feathers
from his hair
And at the Nymphenburger castle
he lays me on the steps
that are icy with cold

7. Munich, Ainmillerstrasse

JAPPES: (*Reads.*) 'Cleopatra seduced Antony
on a ship made of cedarwood
Her throne was ringed
with incense burners
On the walls of her chamber
hung nets full of roses
Every part of her body
was bathed in different oils...'

LUISE: Jappes...

JAPPES: Listen to me
　　　You have a lot to learn
　　　A convent teaches you nothing
　　　about life
　　　Not even the look in your eyes is feminine

LUISE: But your look has hypnotised me
　　　I convinced myself
　　　that I'd got used to this town
　　　I walked like a huge statue of liberty
　　　through the crowds of people
　　　coming and going to work
　　　But as soon as the will left me
　　　and I let my arms drop to my sides
　　　the first man to see me caught me
　　　and reeled me in
　　　It was at least an Indian
　　　living in the Ainmillerstrasse

JAPPES: Don't act
　　　like you were standing outside in the wind
　　　with me
　　　with snot dripping from your nose

LUISE: I know
　　　You're thoughtful
　　　You'd wrap bandages round the trees
　　　after you'd cut their branches off

JAPPES, offended, switches the sun lamp off.

　　　I don't want to know
　　　how you got hold of that thing
　　　or who you stole the new suitcase from

JAPPES: I'm glad you reminded me
　　　I have to go travelling for a bit

He goes to the door.

LUISE: Stay

JAPPES: I can't
It's midnight already

LUISE: The night creatures are going hunting

JAPPES: This time it's me being hunted

LUISE: Stay

JAPPES: You take me to the same street lamps
that I lay under yesterday

LUISE: See you tomorrow

JAPPES: Tomorrow I'll be in Paris
I'll write

LUISE: I let myself be captured by a man
my first
and now he's gone
The flying Dutchman
with his shady business deals
and his bad novel
has lit a little fire
and I'll be busy for a while
trying to put it out

8. Munich, Steinecksaal

Carnival. People dressed as pirates and sea captains, paper streamer snakes, water snakes. LUISE is dressed as a mermaid. She sits on Bruno FRANK's shoulders.

FRANK: This is the woman
with the most beautiful breasts
in central Europe

FEUCHTWANGER: I thought she was the princess on the pea

FRANK: I'm not a pea
Feuchtwanger
I'm a chilli pepper

He lets LUISE slide on to FEUCHTWANGER's lap.

FRANK: 'Drink up the pleasure
      lucky children.
      Soon it will run dry
      Don't look forwards
      don't look back
      Kiss fleetingly
      Be carefree
      Enjoy the moment'

FEUCHTWANGER: Bullshit

FRANK: Wedekind

FEUCHTWANGER: Will you dance

LUISE: I can't touch the ground

FRANK: She's sewn in
      She has to be carried

FEUCHTWANGER strokes the grey fish tail.

LUISE: It's my convent school uniform
      There wasn't enough to make scales for my breasts
      And what are you going as

FEUCHTWANGER: I'm going as a poet

FRANK: Me too

He goes.

LUISE: Would you read my manuscripts?

FEUCHTWANGER: As long as you're not too sensitive

LUISE: I'm not

FEUCHTWANGER: Then let's do it

He lets her slide off his lap.

LUISE: I can't touch the ground

FEUCHTWANGER catches her again.

33

9. Munich, Ainmillerstrasse

Candles on the ground. LUISE burns her manuscripts.

LUISE: Today is my birthday
      Baptism of fire
      What will be left
      will anything be left

      Bullshit
      He said bullshit
      Expressionist bullshit
      If you're twenty-two
      Feuchtwanger said
      you can get away with that sort of thing
      But today's my birthday
      so everything must go
      I can see
      nothing is substantial
      nothing resists
      everything flies
      of its own accord
      into the flame
      everything
      Father's wedding announcement
      Not that I care
      that my stepmother
      is the same age as me
      Here they are
      the letters from the Indian
      'My dearest Lu
      I owe you a lot of...
      My little one
      I'll be travelling to Germany soon...'
      I owe you a lot of...
      Go
      Travel
      You'll never arrive

How beautifully the words burn
They sigh just a tiny bit
before they give themselves to the fire
Little burns
little wounds
wonderful
to begin again naked and new
and real

She sneezes.

Pollen smoke
Fire smoke
Book smoke

She burns herself. The writing desk catches fire.

I'm not made of paper

The door opens. A GIRL appears, holding her apron together at the front.

LUISE: Did the Good Lord send you

GIRL: Lion sent me
With a complimentary ticket

From the apron fall apples, bread, coffee beans. LUISE snaps out of her trance, starts to put out the fire, rescues a manuscript.

10. Munich, Georgenstrasse

Lion FEUCHTWANGER's house. Stones are being thrown at the window. BRECHT throws a plant pot out.

BRECHT: Time to shoot back

FEUCHTWANGER: This is my house poet
He's up and coming.
Even though the theatre here
has just removed his play from the programme

BRECHT: So

FEUCHTWANGER: Our currency has galloping consumption
    By the time the royalties came along
    they weren't worth a stitch

BRECHT: So

FEUCHTWANGER: The actors get paid in the morning
    and run straight to the shops
    to swap their money for food
    By the afternoon it's worthless

LUISE says nothing.

BRECHT: You don't talk much

FEUCHTWANGER: But after 'Drums in the Night'
    she ran about for hours
    in the freezing cold
    She was iridescent

MARTA FEUCHTWANGER: The title was mine
    Before that it was called 'Spartacus'
    With that title
    you might as well just put a gun to your head

FEUCHTWANGER: My wife is your good angel
    Brecht
    Have you thanked her

BRECHT: My thanks
    is the fact that I took up her suggestion

A man with a hat appears at the window.

MAN: There's been a coup
    Hitler's taken control
    They're arresting prominent Jews
    Take our bikes
    Leave the town
    from the other side

FEUCHTWANGER: Not tonight
    We're too tired
    It'll calm down soon

*The FEUCHTWANGERS go to bed. BRECHT picks up a
guitar and sings to LUISE: Baal songs.*

LUISE: He's badly brought up
    unwashed
    His suit looks as if
    it's been slept in
    So
    I'm wild about him
    He's happened to me
    He is a lion tamer
    A potency
    Pointed cheekbones
    Face of a bird
    small and slender
    His voice
    has no volume
    but a tone
    like buzzing heat
    Brecht and I
    are not alike
    but we have things in common
    He comes from a provincial town
    like me
    His mother is dead
    my mother is dead
    He began doing puppet shows
    I began doing puppet shows
    But I charged one Pfennig
    and he charged two Marks
    half the day's wage of a worker
    Which tells you something

11. Augsburg, Bleichstrasse

BRECHT: This room has four empty chairs
    But you have to sit on me

LUISE: There's no chair for me

BRECHT: How perceptive
        The first one is the afternoon nap chair
        the second is the reading chair
        the third is the commode
        the fourth is the brandy drinking chair
        You drink too much

LUISE: On the first one there's Bi
        on the second Marianne
        on the third one Helene
        on the fourth one…

BRECHT: They should all have been called Marie

He takes the bottle away from her.

LUISE: My heart is always busy
        my liver should be kept busy too

BRECHT: You're too heavy for me

LUISE: I'm not heavy

BRECHT: Your head weighs
        as much as a small child

LUISE: Actually you're a nice person
        But you don't let yourself
        Be nice
        You'd like to be a tartar
        riding around with a lump of raw flesh
        under your saddle
        rubbing it tender as you go
        But you're just from Augsburg
        So you have to pretend to be coarse

BRECHT: And you're from Ingolstadt
        And you want to do things that men do
        You want to be recognised for things that men do
        and you want them to tell you you have beautiful eyes
        You can't have both

The way you are
no man could ever lose himself in you
There's not enough empty space

I'm on my way
I can't be held
Tomorrow I'll be
back in the Kantstrasse
No woman
ever died of crying

LUISE: I'll stuff bread into my ears
My mother kissed holes
in my face
I'll fill them all up
And offer him smooth skin

And when I cut off my heels
no shoes will fit me
to run along beside him
where he walks with his giant's boots

A night
like a poem
A levitation
I float
I fly
But he's not looking

She floats.

12. Ingolstadt, Kupfergasse

LUISE: Cold homecoming in Ingolstadt
This time everybody's looking

The SISTERS are sitting side by side on a bench.

FATHER: I'm paying out
and I want to see some return
Results

Diplomas
A middle school teacher
at the very least

LUISE: I don't need qualifications to write

FATHER: What ideas have you got

LUISE: Some

FATHER: Not many of them look like jobs

LUISE: But
I've been published

FATHER: You've been published
And how many Pfennigs did it cost

LUISE: But

FATHER: Versailles ruined us
We've been a garrison town
since 1870
With no soldiers
there's no growth
Only losses
stripping all of us bare

LUISE: But

FATHER: I wanted all my children
to be able to study
Inflation is eating up their future

LUISE: But

FATHER: We've taken food from our mouths
to help you climb the ladder
and you sit there in the cellar
like there's a halo on your head
That's over now

LUISE: But
I can't stay here

FATHER: You haven't touched your drink
    Do you think the coffee
    grows in the pot
    It has to be bought
    and it has to be drunk
    I can't give you any more money

LUISE: Then I will have to stay here

13. Ingolstadt, Kupfergasse

LUISE on a train. FATHER with two letters in his hand.

FATHER: Dear father
    A miracle
    I'm to be performed
    A Mr Seeler
    is putting on my play
    Now I must jump off this train

The sisters read.

SISTERS: 'To Marieluise Fleisser
    Ingolstadt
    Dear Miss Fleisser
    As regards the title of the piece
    none of us were very keen on
    "Purgatory" "Souls in Purgatory" etc
    We have a much more ingenious idea
    that really excited us all
    and we do hope that you'll agree
    Namely "Purgatory in Ingolstadt"'

FATHER: Why Ingolstadt

SISTERS: 'That title
    went down well with a lot of people'
    Open brackets 'Such as Ihering
    Dr Feuchtwanger
    Brecht etc' close brackets

41

'As I said
it seems to all of us
that the title is extraordinarily auspicious
Unfortunately I've been so busy
I didn't get the chance
to write to you sooner
but I took the liberty
of publicising the play in the newspapers
under that name
in the hope that
I could count on your authorisation
after the fact
As regards your coming here
that must be made possible at all costs
I found out about the trains from Ingolstadt today
The best thing would be for you to
take the express passenger train
which leaves Ingolstadt at 9.39 in the morning
and arrives in Berlin at 11.50 in the evening
A third class ticket costs 29 Marks 80
For the moment I am sending you 50 Marks
We also need to establish
a means of recognising each other'
open brackets
'as Dr Feuchtwanger is travelling to Spain tomorrow
and the next day'
close brackets
'Perhaps we might each have a white handkerchief
over our arm
or something

Kindly confirm this with me before you leave
Let's settle with a white handkerchief
over the right arm
I am quite small and broad
with black horn-rimmed glasses
Warm wishes
Seeler'

FATHER: Hopefully she'll give him a wide berth

SISTERS: 'PS don't worry
      about your clothes
      They're really of no great importance'

They open a second letter.

LUISE'S VOICE: '28th April 1926
      Dear Father
      Success
      The production
      will not make a Pfennig
      even the actors
      are working on the Jung stage
      for free
      just to get known
      But now I can get a contract
      with a publisher
      and a fixed monthly salary
      In the Autumn I will
      definitely have to come back to Berlin for a while
      On the journey here
      I was very ill
      For the whole ten hours
      I had uninterrupted nausea and a high fever
      When I come back I'll take
      the fast train
      I was ill for three days
      they had to drag me out of bed to rehearsals
      I don't know whether anyone in Ingolstadt
      has seen the reviews'

SISTERS: Of course we have
      An Alfred Kerr writes
      'Fleisser has natural talent
      if she actually exists
      and it isn't a pseudonym for Brecht
      The Ingolstadt of this piece
      is more vivid than his Augsburg

the first two acts have a power
which Brecht
with his careful spinning
of shimmering
synthetic threads
has never yet achieved'

LUISE'S VOICE: Can you believe it Father
he's praising me
above Brecht

SISTERS: 'If an Anneluise Fleisser actually exists'

LUISE: Marieluise
They'll have to start getting that right

SISTER: 'She seems to be
an observer
a capturer
of nature
not a tired imitator
but a scrupulous documenter
of predatory small town humanity'

LUISE'S VOICE: 'In any case the performance of my play
was the first one in the Jung Theatre
at which there wasn't an outbreak of boos and hisses
and a hail of rotten fruit
Near me only two people booed
I've had to hire a suit
They told me when I got here
that I couldn't be seen in public
looking the way I did
Must stop now
What's going on at home'

FATHER: Our name's in the paper now

SISTER 1: She's a pioneer

SISTER 2: What a pity it's in Berlin

SISTER 1: Imagine
>if she'd got a rotten egg
>right in the face

SISTER 2: Or even worse
>on her hired suit

SISTER 1: Theatre can be dangerous

14. Berlin, Bluthner-Saal concert hall

LUISE: It's as if I've been dropped
>From the moon
>Onto the street
>cripples
>blind people
>lame people
>tinkers
>open suitcases
>Everything for sale
>On the stage
>a woman
>half naked
>dressed in red
>golden ankle chains
>red lipsticked belly button
>powdered body
>beckoning fingers
>open thighs

ANITA BERBER dances her 'Morphium' dance.

MAN: It's unbelievable
>She's shameless
>A goddess of the gutter

SEELER: An age without illusions
>wants its female bodies
>stripped naked too

BRECHT: A woman
    who pointed at her once
    got half her finger bitten off

MAN: She's got a bad reputation all over the world

SEELER: She's just in fashion

LUISE smokes a cigar.

BRECHT: You didn't expect it did you
    that you could be successful with a small town play
    in a metropolis like this
    That's a fate beyond what you could read
    in the lines of your palm
    Tonight you're going to be in paradise
    with me

SEELER: Why don't you write
    a comic play
    about your home town
    I'm sure you'd be good at that

LUISE smokes.

BRECHT: Drink
    The cognac's on the publishers
    'I like a woman with appetites'

SEELER: Why don't you write
    a comic play
    about your home town

LUISE sinks more and more deeply into the chair.

    You know I wanted to do
    a young man's play
    But Brecht said
    you're not doing his play
    You're doing Fleisser's
    The young man
    blasted a bullet through his lung

LUISE: I feel sick
     I have to throw up

    BRECHT opens LUISE's handbag, she throws up into it.

MAN: First the woman takes the cognac
     then the cognac takes the woman

BRECHT: Did you have to tell her that

SEELER: But it's the truth

BRECHT: You know nothing about people
     Or about theatre

SEELER: You ungrateful…
     I'll wipe that smile…

    BRECHT slaps him round the face with a napkin.
    LUISE doubles over with pain.

LUISE: I have to go home

BRECHT: I'll take you

LUISE: I mean Ingolstadt
     I can't live here

BRECHT: You've got a publishing contract
     You're not a woman
     who has to work the streets for a living

LUISE: I'm gaining nothing

BRECHT: You always gain something
     Sometimes it's only experience

LUISE: I'm just passing through

BRECHT: You never give your opinion

LUISE: People make me tired

BRECHT: Fine
     go back to the provinces

Write invisible words
Organise your own obscurity

15. Ingolstadt, Kupfergasse

LUISE: But in Ingolstadt
I wrote a new play
about soldiers who build a bridge
And I have a new love affair
with a Danube swimmer
and owner of a tobacco shop

I have to go to Berlin
Brecht wants to direct the play
under a pseudonym
It's entirely his suggestion
He clicks his fingers
and I go

Your roots are here
says my Danube swimmer
Trees have roots I say
People have legs
I can't bear blows like a boxer
I'm not a person
who could build themselves a bamboo tent
in any corner of the world
But I have written a new play
and I'm not a china goose above a mantelpiece
I want to fly
Then fly
says Bepp the Danube swimmer
and puts an engagement ring on my finger
I want the far away
in all its farness
to be close to me
I will miss him
Bepp is the best

But not to marry
'Darling sweet child
Dearest daughter of sorrow'
He'll write to me every day
'Your place is beside me
in the shop
You don't have to do anything but write
just sit at the counter and write
under the boxes of Havana cigars
He believes his happiness
Is in Ingolstadt

But I must to go to Berlin
Brecht's already rehearsing my play

16. Berlin, Schiffbauerdamm Theatre

Empty theatre canteen.

LUISE: The rehearsal was a crucifixion

BRECHT: Only the worst is good enough

LOUDSPEAKER: Five minute call

LUISE: I can't stay any more

BRECHT: Fear is there
        to be conquered

LUISE: You're out for scandal
       at my cost
       You're pouring petrol
       over every scene
       On the opening night
       I'll be a nervous wreck
       It's me who'll get the slating
       not you

BRECHT: Mater dolorosa

LUISE: I need some orange peel

BRECHT: Try China

LUISE: A little voice is telling me I need orange peel
or I'll get a fever

LOUDSPEAKER: Company to the stage for scene five

BRECHT: Just the end to do now

LUISE: You won't find it by rushing

BRECHT: I'll whip it into shape

LUISE: It's not my play anyway
It was your idea
It's nothing to do with me
It's not one of my themes

BRECHT: I hacked out a path for you
I set up your trapeze wire
and now you're too frightened
to get any higher than your high heeled shoes
What do you want

LUISE: Orange peel

LOUDSPEAKER: Mr Brecht to the stage

BRECHT exits.

LUISE: Of course I'm right
The critics will annihilate me
The Deutsche Zeitung will write
'The writer hopes to use Ingolstadt
to explore certain atavistic emotional impulses
but becomes impossibly mired
in her own primeval sexual swamp
This is probably an unfortunate result
of the play being written by a woman'

The earth will shake
There'll be an explosion

a stoning
an insurrection
German nationalists
will spit at me
for being a woman
My father will despair
I'll have brought shame
on the family
I will be barred from the house
I never want to see Brecht again
I never want to see Brecht again
I never want to see Brecht again

III. In the Belly of the Fish

17. Berlin, Barfussgasse

LUISE: I sit plucked on my perch
in the Barfussgasse
waiting for rescue
A fish comes along
and swallows me immediately
My mother's voice
warns me in vain

Draws is a journalist
a poet
a right wing nationalist
and an enemy of Brecht's

Brecht marries Helene
I get engaged to Draws

'Vi hava förlovat oss och gladjas
At att därum kunna undervätta vänner
Och bekanta'

I agreed to the engagement
although I'm already engaged
I'll have to disengage
and let my Danube swimmer float away

A curtain of cloud
I shiver to my bones
It rains
rains anvils
A man who'll stand by me
who'll kiss me in the street
That's what I long for
'Be careful what you wish for
it might come true'

His is the kiss
of a fish
A deep sea fish
A fish that was never in Noah's ark
He keeps a jungle creature
A flying mongoose
To bite me in the leg
At times like this out on the balcony
because I'm smoking while I hang up the washing

And to eat up Brecht's letters
so I can't read them
not even once

DRAWS: Why don't you change publishers

LUISE: You can't dictate my every move

DRAWS: Every breath

LUISE: You're supporting your mother
with my money

DRAWS: Only when she needs it

LUISE: You're a fish that only
takes for itself

DRAWS: You can leave

LUISE: I can't leave
because I've got a stone in my shoe
that I can't escape
All of this has happened
because I need to feel something else
more than I feel that stone

DRAWS: The Brecht stone

18. Spain, Beach

LUISE: I travel with Draws to Sweden

to Andorra
to Barcelona
Spain is beautiful
Spanish men are beautiful
Most of all, the sea is beautiful
It doesn't need a nationality
I bow before the sea
for the first time and the last
el mar
la mer
das Meer
the sea
'I want to scratch the water
bite it
grip it
The wind wants to eat me
The sun wants to eat me'
Sight and hearing have flown
'The wind blasts the sand onto our damp skin
so we get a new hard skin of sand'

I want to take all the shells home with me

DRAWS: I'll let you take twelve

LUISE: Three hundred

DRAWS: Let's go to the café
The more often we go
the less he charges

LUISE: I'll cover my body
with two hundred big shells
so I'm a shell woman

DRAWS lies on top of LUISE.

The edges cut into my skin

DRAWS: What good is your armour now
Let's go to the place

where they cut off the pieces of eel
like slices of sausage
I'll make a command bridge
on the terrace
You can wear a pirate's kerchief
and sweep the walkers away
with a broom

LUISE: Galatea drives past in a carriage made of shells
The mermaids have been stewed
Tomorrow I'll be back
in my furnished room in 7 Barfussstrasse
in Berlin

19. Berlin, Barfussstrasse

DRAWS: You have to earn money

LUISE: I'll write a novel in a year

DRAWS: That's not enough

LUISE: I'll write lying down
without a desk
on the backs of bills
till my hand shakes
Why don't you write any more

DRAWS: 'My pores suffer from a pressure
that others do not feel'
the pressure of the deep sea

LUISE: You give out electric shocks
They paralyse me

DRAWS: 'Your will will desert you
You will no longer be you
I will suck you up'

She is silent.

Speak
Why do you speak
when I haven't asked you anything
Why are you always next to me
Go away
Why are you not next to me
can't you see
I'm suffering
I warned you about me

You're getting thinner all the time
and translucent like a fishbone

LUISE: I can't do this any more
        I'm going to jump out of the window

DRAWS: Wait till I'm out of the room
        or they'll say I pushed you

He exits.

LUISE: Now I can't do it
        I can't fit through the window
        I'm so puffed up with hate

IV. A Time in Shelter

20. Ingolstadt, Kupfergasse

LUISE: I wake up in a different dream
I'm sitting in my parents' house
in a collar made of bone lace
counting the days
on my fingers
dull like lead
The newspapers
don't want my writing now
I don't fit the ideal
of national socialist womanhood
I'm the failure
spat at by the world
and hiding
back in her father's house
I've come full circle
only to see
That the wide wide world
only has a narrow space
For me

Next to me sits
the abhorrent void
On the bed
in the kitchen
When it comes to business
there's an old pioneer
who shakes his head and says
'If that Fleisser woman comes near
I'll break her in two'
'Build the town a swimming pool'
says Bepp the Danube swimmer
'Then they'll forgive you'

Feuchtwanger and Brecht
have left the country
I need the nearness of Bepp
The bills are coming in
It's reckoning time
He's a business man
I can be a business woman
I can surprise them
I can be a wife
in a four postered marriage bed
with a skylight to see the sky
Disappointment is like a spider
crouching on my head
I'm no longer Bepp's sweet child
Now he calls the shots
I threw his love back in his face
I swallowed his engagement ring
Now I want him back
A last refuge

21. Tobacconist's shop, Ingolstadt

BEPP: The man
puts the woman behind the counter
And the state
puts the man
behind the front line
to fight for his country

BEPP dictates to LUISE who writes in an exercise book.

Business duties
1. Cashing up
2. Book keeping
3. Day book
4. Account payments
5. Bills

Write up the payments from the day before
in the yellow bills book

Accounts that haven't been paid remain open
Accounts that are paid get the annotation 'pd'

When necessary transfer information
from the yellow bills book into the accounts book
Accounts are held by
Witmann the barber
Mrs Karl
Mrs Euringer
The rowing club
Those with accounts
must also be entered in the day book
Records are kept in the accounts book
in the following order: date, number, amount
Make ticks on the left and the right
when paid
On the left record debt
on the right calculate credit

You can still write at night
I'm with the anti-aircraft defence
I go into the centre
of the blaze

LUISE: After the shop I go home
I'm tired
But I keep myself busy
'Because I can no longer read
I can no longer do anything to fill myself up
A ghost sucks everything away'
I have lost
Surrendered
I'm at the end
This is my end

I see the Literary Establishment come dancing past
all buttoned up in tie and tails
a women on his left arm and another on his right
No room
he shouts

LITERARY ESTABLISHMENT: No room

LUISE: The Danube dances past
      in a wide blue hoop skirt

DANUBE: Come to my arms
      I've always got room for you
      beside the melted snow and ice

LUISE dances with the DANUBE.

LUISE: It feels good
      but I can't die yet
      I have to write

*LUISE dances on alone, dances into the arms of a straightjacket
which is held out by two men.*

DOCTOR: A little white pill
      which makes everything smaller
      the fear
      the pain
      the person
      the memories
      Take a handful every day
      And in three months you can
      leave our institution
      and be back with your Havana boxes

22. Ingolstadt, Skyline

Air raid siren.

CHORUS: She must do her war duty

      Her name is on the black list

      On Saturdays
      she must scrub the factory floor

      On her knees

On her knees
In front of the picture of Hitler
with no glass in it

Using a pipette
she must measure out molten metals
calculate the correct composition of steel

She must get nothing wrong

That would be sabotage

She must not have a headache
and get the numbers mixed up

That would be sabotage

Chrome, nickel, manganese

She must stare into the mouth of the cannon

She must stare into the mouth of war

She must not make a mistake

That would be sabotage

LUISE: But of course I've got a headache
a constant headache
It's the grip
of the angel of history

CHOIR: Early warning siren

Warning siren

Low flying planes

In Hamburg
roofs fly through the air

The asphalt bubbles

The dead fall
on top of the dead from the day before

The streets are deserts

40 per cent of the town of Ingolstadt is destroyed

The Americans move in
They shoot the crocodile

We open the blackout curtains

May the eighth

The war is over

Bells ring

We drink to death

LUISE: I have survived
    the war and what came after
    double occupation of the flat
    arrest for black marketeering
    surgery on my heart

    I have survived
    I'm alive somehow
    existing somewhere
    between memory and aphasia
    A woman without influence
    A woman without words
    A woman who prefers to stay quiet

    In the blacksmith's house
    they eat with wooden spoons
    I know the look
    in the exhausted eyes around me
    Life punishes those
    who push too far
    is what it says

    At some point
    I forgot my old existence
    At some point
    I forgot

that I'm a writer
At some point
a long time ago
the world forgot me

But in the last act
I'm touched by grace
one more time
In my advancing years
I'm given the gift of sons
I don't even know
if I want them
But they want me
They've chosen me
And they're hungry
for the taste of my words
The curtain opens again
I'm back on stage

It goes on
I dance again
I still have time
The public crowds in
We need chairs
More chairs

She dances with three puppets under her arm: RAINER, MARTIN, FRANZ-XAVER.[1]

---

1 *Translator's note:* Rainer Werner Fassbinder, Martin Sperr, Franz Xaver Kroetz, Marieluise Fleisser's 'adopted sons' who championed her work at the end of her life.

THE TIME OF THE TORTOISE

The play draws on themes from the story So heiss, so kalt, so hart *(So hot, so cold, so hard) by Hassouna Mosbahi.*

The translator would like to thank Sylviana Ollennu and all at the Goethe Institute for making the translation of this play possible.

Characters

SAMI

ALI

ULU

THE WOMAN

THE MOTHER

JOURNALISTS, POLICE, PEOPLE, OLD WOMAN

The play takes place in Southern Europe.

One

Greenhouse made of plastic sheeting.

Day.

Two bodies lie on stacking pallets. JOURNALISTS pull down the plastic sheets that cover them, take lots of photos.

ALI sits up.

ALI: No photos please

SAMI: Same here

ALI: I don't want
      my family finding out from the newspaper

SAMI: Not in this place
      And definitely not with Ali
      Not now
      when I can't defend myself anymore

The photographers leave.

ALI: YOU were my downfall

SAMI: YOU

ALI: YOU

SAMI: I told you
      if you didn't watch out
      something would happen

ALI: The end came between cucumbers and courgettes

SAMI: They're waiting
      for us to harvest them

ALI: Looking forward to our hands

SAMI: I see no sign

that death has any meaning at all

ALI: Why should it
        When life doesn't

SAMI: If I'd never met you
        I'd have found something
        some meaning

ALI: Sami

SAMI: If I'd never met you

ALI: I wanted to be your friend
        from the minute I saw you

SAMI: It was Autumn
        Harvest time

ALI: One look was enough

SAMI: There was one harvest
        in our village
        Not for every year like here

ALI: Everyone was happy
        Except you

SAMI: The older boys
        ran from one wedding to the next

ALI: Searching
        for eyes soft like velvet

SAMI: I was ten
        I lay alone under the olive tree
        and dreamed
        dreamed of the world
        of the cities
        I would be in one day
        of the women
        I would meet one day
        Then your shadow fell over me

ALI: You were alone
       I was alone too
       They used to hit you
       because you read books
       Instead of working

SAMI: I was always getting hit
       I don't know what for any more

ALI: Because you were different
       from the rest

SAMI: My parents told me
       three things are haram[1]
       Blood
       Ashes
       and YOU and your family
       You of all people
       wanting to be my friend

ALI: I gave you a wonderful idea

SAMI: It took everything I had

ALI: Maktub[2]

SAMI: Mountains of cakes
       Sweets
       White bread
       That's what we were going to eat
       when we went looking for a tortoise
       You made me believe
       that for a tortoise
       we would get half the world

ALI: We ran and ran
       we ran around for a whole day
       till we found it
       The giant tortoise

1 Taboo
2 Fate

SAMI: And the beating
　　　My father beat me half to death
　　　All for a couple of sweets

ALI: But we were in the town
　　　All alone
　　　we saw the souk

SAMI: He beat me half to death

ALI: And me he threw in the dirt
　　　like a cigarette butt
　　　but we were in the town

SAMI: If you'd never happened
　　　he'd have let me go to secondary school

ALI: You'd have been left behind

SAMI: I'd have become a professor
　　　I'd have made my family proud

ALI: Your mother
　　　broke my index finger

SAMI: My mother always
　　　warned me about you

ALI: And
　　　didn't you hear her this time

SAMI: Perhaps she was in the hamam[3]

ALI: My mother died in the hamam
　　　They carried her home
　　　There was a white sheet on the ground
　　　And she was under it
　　　The relatives
　　　who stood around the cactus bush
　　　took her away on their shoulders
　　　I didn't see
　　　when they threw the sand on her

3　Bath-house

SAMI: That's why you'd never believe
   She was dead
   My mother won't believe it either
   About me

ALI: My father took a present to the woman next door
   straight away
   A whole casket of sugar

SAMI: What was he supposed to do
   He needed a woman

ALI: I stole a bit of it
   A really tiny bit
   And she told on me
   She didn't want me

SAMI: She had a star
   tattooed on her forehead

ALI: They had children again
   Far too many
   Far too many
   for us to ever feel full
   We had no vegetables
   Nothing

SAMI: You've had enough now
   The vegetables for half the population of Europe
   have been through our hands

ALI: Later I thought
   the town would rescue me
   But then the film was over
   and my luck was over too

SAMI: You enticed me with the cinema
   Enticed me into the town

ALI: 'Once Upon A Time In the West'
   How often did we see that
   Endless times

73

Dreamed about
how we'd come back to the village
stand in the middle of the square
play the death tune
draw our pistols
And then everyone
who'd tormented us
would fall to the ground
like yellow leaves

SAMI: You can't pull the trigger
         when your index finger's broken

ALI: But my heart wasn't broken then

SAMI: We had nothing
         No money
         No prospects
         You dragged me down

ALI: I dragged you out

SAMI: To the bars
         To the railway stations

ALI: One day you disappeared
         Just like that
         One day there, the next day gone
         Without a trace
         I resigned myself to it
         at some point
         and then
         you crossed my path again
         and I couldn't shake you off

SAMI: YOU couldn't shake ME off?

ALI: I paid a fortune
         to smuggle myself
         on the ferry to Europe
         and then I found you
         seasick

ALI: Be glad
       that you found me
       You've worked under plastic
       lived under plastic
       My body gave you
       The only human warmth you got
       The people here don't value us
       'They eat with their hands
       they steal'
       they say
       'We don't want them in our bars'
       They've forgotten
       how poor they were
       before they built the greenhouses

SAMI: If you'd never happened
       my whole life would have been different
       And my death wouldn't have happened
       amongst dogs
       and jam jars
       and pepper rinds
       and clingfilm
       In a foreign land
       Where I'm an illegal

ALI: We're dead
       If tomorrow
       they started selling visas in the supermarket
       it wouldn't matter to us
       Now we're dead we're legal
       easy as that

   A WOMAN comes up to them.

       She's not even blonde

   SAMI says nothing.

       She could at least be blonde
       But anyway
       You screwed her in her kitchen

from behind
and lit candles
so I could see your shadows
I stood outside on the street
I followed you
I saw
the shadow of a giantess
fat thighs
big behind

SAMI: The kitchen's got no curtains
It's not my fault
her kitchen's got no curtains

My parents are religious
they're waiting
for me to bring home a daughter in law

I want children
I want grandchildren
I want a family

ALI: I'm your family
Our eyes have seen
the same sun
the same olive trees
the same camels
We know what we mean

SAMI: She wanted me
She really wanted me
She wanted to go travelling with me

ALI: If you've got money
you get friends
But you've got no money
financial arrangements
travel arrangements
sexual arrangements
they're all connected
don't kid yourself

And she's not even blonde

SAMI: She's got beautiful feet
I can see everything in feet
Whether a woman's young or old
willing or unwilling

ALI: She shows her legs to everyone
up to the crotch
and you're looking at her feet

*An OLD WOMAN comes up to them, pulls the younger
WOMAN away, spits on SAMI's body.*

SAMI: You made a mistake

ALI: You made two

SAMI: They're blaming all of us
for something you did
all on your own
'They're murderers'
they say
'They're violent
And now they've
committed suicide side by side...'

ALI: The police shot us

SAMI: No one'll admit to that
They'll say
'Now they've committed suicide
side by side
but soon they'll
get hold of our daughters
and murder them'

ALI: Their jails are full to bursting
with their own people

A POLICEMAN brings a black man in.

POLICEMAN: Are these your friends

ULU: I don't know them

ALI: Liar

SAMI: He knows you in the biblical sense

ULU and the POLICEMAN go.

ALI: He came along the street
with a suitcase on his head

SAMI: You picked him up in the bar

ALI: He ran right into me
he shone

SAMI: You went after him

ALI: Because you treated me
like a bag of cement

SAMI: I shared everything with you

ALI: You stopped sharing your sweat

SAMI: You were greedy
too greedy for everything

ALI: So
I just desire more
than you
than my father
than my grandfather
I would have liked to go to a dentist
Without gaps in my teeth
I could have started a new life

SAMI: Because of the gaps in your teeth
we're dead

ULU turns back to look at them from far away.

SAMI: I wish you'd stayed
in the belly of Africa

ALI: He was desperate
      for me to let him drive the car
      That was his dream
      His house was an old banger
      that didn't go

SAMI: As soon as I saw the car
      it was clear to me
      Doesn't it look like a tortoise
      I said to you

ALI: A German car

SAMI: A tortoise on wheels

ALI: An old model

SAMI: Can you drive
      I asked you
      Of course
      Have you got a licence
      Of course not

ALI: Where's a Beduin
      supposed to take a driving test

SAMI: It was clear to me
      That this time the tortoise
      wouldn't just break an index finger
      it'd break our necks

ALI: A simple exchange

SAMI: A drug exchange
      A tortoise with
      a stomach full of poison
      If you're illegal
      you're not meant to do illegal things

ALI: If you're illegal
      everything's illegal
      so it doesn't matter

what you do

SAMI: You've got other people on your conscience

ALI: You know
      that I'd never take that kind of drug
      I don't even eat over-ripe figs
      because they're practically alcohol

      But if other people want it
      want a rush
      need it even
      why should I object

      And if they want to die of it
      that's their problem
      They've paid for it haven't they

SAMI: It was cut with something
      contaminated

ALI: I don't think so

SAMI: Don't talk yourself out of it

ALI: Do you think
      you can get rich from tomatoes
      Do you think
      tomatoes can buy you
      a flat with a front door
      instead of a shack made of plastic sheets

SAMI: You've forgotten something

ALI: What

SAMI: We don't need a front door anymore

ALI: How do you know
      that stuff wasn't pure

Two

Greenhouse.

Night.

The WOMAN stands beside SAMI.

WOMAN: A woman can no more trust a man
   than a sieve can hold water

SAMI: Why don't you say 'an Arab man'

WOMAN: That was never the problem
   The problem was your friend
   I told you
   He wasn't good for you

ALI: Don't let this lady talk you round

WOMAN: I'm not a lady
   I'm not one of those
   whose nails go with her shoes
   whose lipstick matches her hat
   But I know
   which man is my perfect match
   And you were a match for me
   Even your hair
   matched the throwover on my sofa

SAMI: I wish you'd brought it
   Do I have to lie under plastic
   till the very end

WOMAN: When my father died
   he lay in cold storage
   no glasses
   no underwear
   no teeth
   and I wished

that they'd
covered him with plastic
at least

SAMI: Plastic is our fate

WOMAN: Working in the plastic factory
gives you a headache

SAMI: The smells

WOMAN: But I pray
I'll be allowed to stay
There's a lot to do
but the new production methods
don't need many workers

SAMI: Plastic only lasts one or two years
If it's very windy
only one
And
there are sixty
unlicensed plastic plantations

WOMAN: That's my hope

SAMI: You need to look for a man
who'll look after you

WOMAN: Don't want to

SAMI: Do you think
the rain will bring you money

WOMAN: It's not raining anymore

SAMI: No

WOMAN: And it's hot
and I'm cold

SAMI: You need a man
to keep you warm

WOMAN: I don't

SAMI: You need one
who'll go travelling with you

WOMAN: I'll be faithful to you
that's my hope

SAMI: You love waste
You leave the light on
in the bedroom
even when you aren't there

WOMAN: And I can stay with you
even when you aren't there

SAMI: I have no strength
to hold you

WOMAN: As long as I keep remembering you

SAMI: Memories get old too
Tomorrow they'll mean nothing

ULU comes up and sits next to ALI on the pallet.

ALI: Ulu!
You're like a light

ULU: I change lightbulbs

ALI: Despite your dark skin

ULU: My dream was
to go to the sea
and now I'm changing lightbulbs
on a restaurant ship

ALI: I worked with the tomatoes
Thirty degrees in the winter
In the hot house
You can't stand up straight
You always have to stoop

ULU: There are
       Two thousand five hundred and seventy eight
       lightbulbs
       on the ship

ALI: You stand straight
       That's why I noticed you
       in the bar
       without a name
       the bar for the Moroccans

SAMI: His moods change
       like the colours of tomatoes

ALI: He's beautiful though
       My eye won't be satisfied
       till he's buried in the ground

SAMI: He's a liar

ALI: I picked him
       from the harvest of heads and bodies
       lined up along the bar

SAMI: He has small ears

ALI: So
       What use are ears
       Can you put things in them

SAMI: It's a sign of a small intelligence

ULU: You insulted my ears
       but forgot my tongue
       I slept with your girlfriend

SAMI: I don't believe that
       She's not even blonde

ULU: But she feels like she is

SAMI: And she doesn't mind
       that those same hands
       stroked Ali

ALI: You
        stroked Ali first too
        and then stroked her

WOMAN: I was sad
        and he comforted me

ALI: A happy accident
        hands reaching out to each other

ULU: She'll get pregnant
        She didn't want any plastic
        to cover my cock

SAMI: A half-caste child
        in these times
        Your mother will stone you

WOMAN: It'll be romantic
        Our love story
        will be filmed
        It'll be seen all over the world
        Do you think
        you're the only sensational news story

SAMI: I would never have imagined it
        Even when you're dead
        the cruelty doesn't stop

WOMAN: You didn't stop
        with your cruelty
        If you hadn't insulted Ulu
        none of this would have come out

ALI: Ulu
        what do you want with this
        bowlegged thing
        who likes to pretend she's stupid
        I chose you

ULU: I'd rather choose
        than be chosen

ALI: Ulu
      don't go

SAMI: They're practically running away

ALI: He's dancing in the street

SAMI: They're insane

ALI: We won't see each other again

ULU: Come on
     run after me

ALI: I'll bite your head off
      and then your ears too

WOMAN: Sami
       I love you

ALI: And then she kisses Ulu
      Women will lie
      as soon as open their mouths
      Be glad
      she's gone
      you'd never have seen through her
      you'd have believed her lies
      I tried to tell you

SAMI: I turned you in
      to the police

ALI: You're lying

SAMI: Because I wanted papers

ALI: You're lying

SAMI: Because I wanted to marry her

ALI: Sami

SAMI: Sorry

ALI: Sami

SAMI: They promised me freedom
and paper

ALI: I don't believe it

SAMI: Her brother's a policeman
He suggested it
He always suspected you
were dealing
He told me
if I gave him a tip off
he'd make it worth my while
I never thought
you'd actually do something like that

ALI: You idiot

SAMI: Why didn't you stay where you were
when they pulled us over

ALI: What would you do
if the police stopped you
with a car full of stuff
Put your foot down and fuck off obviously
Pity the car wasn't a Maserati

SAMI: No

ALI: But why did they shoot you too

SAMI: Haven't a clue

ALI: At least if it had been a fair fight
Nose to nose
a muscular policeman's arm
grabs you by the neck
his sweat mixes
with yours
you breathe each other's breath
But like that
from a distance
from behind

SAMI: Maktub

ALI: And now I can't kill you anymore either

SAMI: A fly's
          landed on my lip

ALI: The law says
          you have to be buried the same day

SAMI: Perhaps this is
          The court

ALI: Which one

SAMI: What would you do
          if today was a normal day

ALI: Suck on a lemon
          or on my thumbs
          Eat rubbish
          chase a cat
          perhaps hold my breath for a bit
          I was always the best
          when it came to holding my breath

SAMI: Perhaps this is
          paradise
          The lemon trees drip
          the moths furl
          and unfurl themselves
          and we can't do anything anymore
          We can't suck the juice out of lemons anymore
          can't break open melons anymore
          just to eat the middle
          because it's the sweetest part

ALI: That's not paradise
          It stinks here

SAMI: Who told you
          paradise doesn't stink

88

ALI: It's not like paradise
        It's like the cinema
        because you can't touch it
        Good Sami
        betrayed bad Ali
        and I can't even slit him open
        Can't even stick a corkscrew in him

SAMI: Perhaps that's it

ALI: I'd never have thought that of you

SAMI: It's always good
        to be underestimated

ALI: If I hadn't helped you
        kicked you into action
        you'd have stuck your head back in every time
        like a tortoise

SAMI: Would you do anything different
        if you could start from the beginning
        would you do anything better

ALI: I'd nick a better car
        Not a rustbucket like that
        that doesn't go

SAMI: But you'd still
        transport the same stuff in it

ALI: Any transport business
        might sometimes move stuff
        that's not totally innocent
        that's not a hundred percent sound
        that's not irreproachable

SAMI: A bang
        They're shooting again
        Another bang

ALI: Can it be true
        that they blew you up

SAMI: Can it be true
        that you got hit by a rotten tomato

ALI: The world's balanced
        on the horns of a bull
        standing with his four hooves on four eggs
        Sometimes the world shifts
        from one horn to the other
        there's a bang
        the equilibrium is disturbed
        Why are you laughing

SAMI: Nothing else can happen to us
        Just think
        of all the things we can't get anymore

ALI: No anthrax

SAMI: No testicular cancer

ALI: No in-growing toenails

SAMI: No tuberculosis

ALI: No kidney disease

SAMI: No kidney cancer

ALI: No polio

SAMI: No Alzheimers

ALI: No coughing fits

SAMI: No choking fits

ALI: No fatal accidents

SAMI: Someone's coming

ALI: Where there's carrion
        you get vultures

SAMI: They don't even knock

ALI: There's no one in

MOTHER: Are you no one

SAMI: Mum!

MOTHER: You're a whole new disappointment to me
          when I thought you were an old one
          You've disturbed my peace

SAMI: What's that wheelbarrow for

MOTHER: I'm taking you home

SAMI: Mum you can't
       They won't let you take a dead body
       across the border

MOTHER: I won't be shamed
         Your father's gone to Mecca
         and you do this to us

ALI: Do you still know me too
       You broke my index finger

MOTHER: That doesn't make you one of us
         Come on Sami
         Do you want to stay in this shit hole

SAMI: Sometimes things work themselves out
       We're rubbish too now

MOTHER: You were always like this
         indifferent
         I told you
         to try and make a go of things
         but your ears were full of sand
         Your cousin was the opposite
         He started with just one machine
         had it going day and night
         and when it broke
         and no electrician came
         he held the wire all night

to keep it working
Would you hold the wire
Not even for an hour
And that's why you're here on the rubbish heap
A man doesn't leave his country
his mother and father
and despite that I gave you
a brand new coin to take with you
with an inscription
and I prayed
for a cloud
to go with you on your journey
and offer you shade
because
because I thought
you were going to paradise
and you'd come back a rich man
and that when I was old
I'd be able to afford
all the top class diseases

SAMI: Shut up Mum

MOTHER: Are you ashamed of me
I can't even afford any teeth

ALI: Yes
missing teeth
can really limit your life

MOTHER: What do you want
To stick to my son all your life
Like a tumour

ALI: I was with him
when he had no family by his side
Better a friend who's with you
than a brother who's far away

MOTHER: A friend!
A sick camel's more like it

SAMI: Mum!

MOTHER: I was in the hamam
Salima slapped the wash cloth
on my back
and suddenly everything was clear
I cried for five whole minutes
over you
and I said to the earth
open your arms for me too
and I invited the whole village
to a funeral service
but they didn't come
so I set out on the road

SAMI: How did you manage to
get here
You've never left the house before

MOTHER: I thought to myself
what use is a house to me
I can't talk to a house
I can assert myself
I've just never done it before
My father used to say
a tent full of girls
is an empty tent
I had to show him just once
that I'm not nothing
Your sister's working now
in a second hand shoe shop
I chose some shoes for myself
and set out on the road

*She takes a small bird out of her pocket, pulls off its feathers
and eats it.*

SAMI: Mum!

MOTHER: I baked a 'judge's ear'
and a 'bride's little finger'

for the journey
but I ate them long ago

*She gets more birds out of her bag. Eats them with the feathers
on, with some ceremony.*

MOTHER: I have to find myself a few more provisions
The journey was exhausting
Do they even have birds here
I hope it's not just decomposing fish
On the quay there were so many men standing around
the seagulls couldn't land

She leaves.

SAMI: Are you thinking
What I'm thinking

ALI: That was a fata morgana

SAMI: But the wheeelbarrow's still there

ALI: Perhaps we're dreaming
a novel in episodes

Three

Greenhouse.

Day/night (both at once, à la Magritte).

ALI: Perhaps we're dreaming
       a novel in episodes

    ULU comes back.

SAMI: Here's the next chapter

ALI: Ulu
       you came back
       You got sick of that woman
       pulling you along behind her
       on a lead
       You tried some of that cake
       but it made you sick
       Things take time

    ULU lies down on top of SAMI.

       Ulu
       what are you doing
       keep the ball low
       are you trying to ruin my evening
       has the moon
       dropped on your head
       Ulu?

SAMI: I'm disintegrating
       If you wait a bit
       there'll be holes all over me where you can get in
       I'll be like the surface of the moon
       covered in craters
       my arse on my stomach
       a fairytale

ULU: I can't wait

SAMI: Please

ULU: She compares me with you
     She doesn't speak
     but she's thinking about you
     She closes her eyes
     and thinks about you
     You're always with us
     So now I'm with you
     my darling

SAMI: Listen
      I don't like men

ALI: You bugger

ULU: Tonight you're my treasure trove
     filled with pure little pieces of happiness

ALI: You bugger

ULU groans.

     Coyote
     If the deal had worked out
     I'd have given you everything
     You wouldn't have had to live in that car
     You could have had a flat
     to live in
     and a car
     to drive

ULU: I can't be bought
     But maybe for a hundred thousand
     I'd have offered you a place
     next to my kneecap
     that belonged only to you
     But it didn't work out did it

ALI: You're a dirty dog stealer

You're like a yapping dog yourself
But you're beautiful

ULU: I know

ALI: And one day
you'll let yourself be paid for it
I wouldn't wait too long if I were you

SAMI: Think about your future
sooner

ULU: Yes
Why didn't I discover you before

ALI: My breath is steady
I can bend my index finger
It isn't stiff
I think that facing the target with
Steady breath
is the most important factor
in achieving a hit

ULU: If you had any breath

SAMI: If you had a weapon

ALI: I'm glad
The deal didn't work out

ULU goes to ALI, kisses him lovingly.

ULU: If you had a weapon

SAMI: If I had a weapon

Boat horn.
ULU separates himself from ALI.

ULU: I have to go to the ship

ALI: Yes
get lost

SAMI: Take a ship to Paris

ALI: Don't send a postcard

ULU: I'm alive
       you see
       I'm alive

ULU leaves.

SAMI: Is it going to go on like this forever
       I don't understand
       Everything begins with nothing
       Then everything turns out bad

ALI: It didn't have to go wrong

SAMI: A dream

ALI: But the dream does exist
       It must be
       somewhere

SAMI: Yes you let it go
       and it's staggering round the world on its own

Noises.

ALI: There's a crisis

SAMI: We're right in the middle of it

ALI: I don't want to see anyone else
       I want a mouth organ

SAMI: They exist somewhere

ALI: I'll play the death tune

SAMI: And they'll all fall to the ground like yellow leaves

ALI: Perhaps those rotten courgette leaves were once...
       something else

SAMI: Rubbish was always once something else

ALI: But we're not rubbish

SAMI: No

ALI: I think we should forgive ourselves
      Us
      and the others

SAMI: You're right

ALI: I'm always right

SAMI: We should give up being right too

*People come, put flowers on the bodies until they practically
disappear under a mountain of flowers.*

JOURNALIST 1: The police have these deaths on their
              conscience

JOURNALIST 2: I photographed it all
              but some things you can't capture on camera
              you just feel

JOURNALIST 1: Their deaths must not be in vain

JOURNALIST 2: They have the desert in their eyes
              why bring the desert here
              we've worked hard
              to create a vegetable garden
              that can feed half the world

JOURNALIST 1: We couldn't harvest everything we sowed
              by ourselves

JOURNALIST 2: They bring racism with them
              When they go away
              racism goes away too

JOURNALIST 1: Their blood wants revenge

ALI: We don't want it

SAMI: No lilies on my face
      I don't like the smell

JOURNALIST 1: The police have burned down the shanty town
It's the law that's illegal
not the people
Next week there's going to be a protest march
converging from all sides of the city
like a star

JOURNALIST 2: Marching in a star
or going round in circles
What's going to happen

JOURNALIST 1: The muslims are in the church

JOURNALIST 2: They'll drag them out

The MOTHER appears.

MOTHER: It's so cramped in here
you get your head stuck

The MOTHER picks up a tomato from the floor and eats it.

SAMI: Mother
I wouldn't eat the tomatoes here
I know
how they're made

The WOMAN appears with a child in her arms.

WOMAN: I found this
Shall I keep it

ALI: A tortoise lays a hundred eggs
Why shouldn't a woman have a child

MOTHER: But it belongs to someone

WOMAN: It was forgotten

SAMI: Keep it

MOTHER: When children are small
they tread on your feet
When they're big
they tread on your heart

SAMI: Keep it
  Or you'll be left
  like a miserable cat
  in an empty flat

WOMAN: A new child
  a new world

The MOTHER brings people to look at them.

MOTHER: This is my son
  a martyr
  I never dreamed
  anything would come of him
  It was worth it after all
  It's a miracle

  A miracle

  You must touch the body

  You must tell him your wishes

  Make requests

  You must

  Touch him

The MOTHER is knocked over by the people crowding in.

MOTHER: I love this country
  but the people jump around like horses

SAMI: They're slipping us notes

ALI: Are we the wailing wall now

SAMI: They don't know
  you can't read

ALI: I still know
  what they say

SAMI: Me too

'Can you please make it
so that he comes back to me
I don't want him
to be happy with someone else
I'd rather he was
unhappy with me'

ALI: 'Can you make it so that
My son falls under a bus
He's going to go to jail
I'd rather he was dead'

SAMI: 'Make it so that
he buys me the ring
but not the cheap one
I wouldn't want him then'

ALI: 'I wish for a motorbike
for my boyfriend
so that I can put my hands over his eyes
on that left-hand bend
you know the one'

SAMI: 'I wish that
your wishes never end
that they become a sea of wishes
and that the sea dries to a bone
before even one of them comes true'

A burning car tyre rolls in.

They're burning everything

ALI: Looks like it

SAMI: The fumes are poisonous
Plastic is poisonous
when it burns
She should go.
She should take the child away

ALI: Which child

SAMI: She found a child

ALI: She can lose it again

WOMAN: You've brought chaos here
        Why couldn't you stay
        Where you came from

SAMI: We have to do something

ALI: We can't do anything
        We're like Hassan
        the deaf mute
        He sees
        his wife deceiving him
        and he can't tell a soul
        He sees
        the blood poisoning
        creeping through his body
        and he knows there's no doctor

SAMI: Don't fall asleep
        don't fall asleep

ALI: We can only sleep

SAMI: I want a nice end
        Ali
        It was nice with you

ALI: I knew it
        You'll know it one day too
        what I always knew

SAMI: Don't forget me

ALI: Ta'ali [4]

SAMI: We'll meet again on the ferry

   SAMI rolls his body off the pallet and puts out the fire.

4   Come